First Kiss

A Romantic Novel That Explores The Transition From A Casual Sexual Relationship To A Deeper Emotional Connection, Set Against The Backdrop Of A Black Couple's Love Story

Jordy van Bogers

The melancholy sound of the violin revealed nothing of the feelings that were coursing through Emily Bawler as she opened her heart and head to her music. She was sitting on the chair's edge with her eyes closed and her back straight. All was black in the studio save for the one light that hung above her head like a halo.

She was surrounded by a cocoon of wonderful yet melancholy songs that nothing and no one could disturb. In a haze, she was lost. A fog carrying confusion and melancholy. Sadness over being lost and perplexed by questions she didn't know the solutions to. Things she would require assistance organizing. Emily remained silent, keeping the violin tucked under her chin, while the final note slowly faded across the strings in a depressing murmur. Her body started to relax after some time, and she allowed the instrument to fall into her lap. A single tear ran down her face as her head lowered.

She asked the empty room in a quiet tone, "What is wrong with me?"

She took a deep breath and brushed away the tear that had slid beneath her chin. She felt a wave of wrath surge inside her as she peered around the dimly lit room. Just like she did every Friday, she had arrived at the studio to practice, and just as before, the piece she was meant to be performing had transformed from a happy love ballet to a melancholy, impassioned appeal. Occasionally, she wouldn't even notice the difference until she finished writing the last note. She didn't like how this situation she was going through was impacting her songs.

She got up and walked over to her violin bag, gently laying the violin and bow on the plush red velvet mattress. She caressed the rich, dark wood with her hands, wishing she could play the notes exactly as they were written on the music sheets, free from the influence of her feelings. She was nearly blinded by the sight of the violin as she gazed down at it.

With a start, she raised her head. "Is there someone present?" she exclaimed.

Laurie answered, "Yeah, it's me Emily," as she turned on the lights. With her ever-present smile, she entered the room with great speed. "We're heading to Diamondz N DA Ruff Café in Jersey over the bridge to have a bite to eat and maybe get a little tipsy." "Perhaps I'll be fortunate," she remarked, wriggling her crimson, arched eyebrows. Are you in? "It's karaoke night with dancing to follow," she grinned.

Emily considered returning home to sulk about her flat, but she wasn't very fond of the idea. It seemed like what she needed—a glass of chilled wine, some food, and belly laughs with her coworkers.

Yes, I'm on board. Allow me to gather my belongings and secure this space.

"Alright, neat," Laurie replied.

Laurie stood by while Emily piled her music sheets into a black leather binder. She picked up the violin off the stool, closed the case, and put on her red jacket.

Walking over to her, Emily responded, "I'm ready."

Together, they made their way out of the classroom after Emily locked the door behind them. She didn't own a car since taking the tube, or Uber was more convenient. Laurie could not imagine her life without her little silver Acura Hybrid and practically lived out of her car.

Emily questioned as she put her violin in the trunk, "Where is everyone?"

Laurie got behind the wheel and got the car going. Emily shut the doors after slipping into the passenger seat.

In Mark's car, they had already departed. Bobby, Karen, and Gail are with him. As she pulled out of the parking lot and into traffic, she remarked, "We'll meet up with them in a minute.

A few people were coming in by the time they crossed the bridge and arrived at the lounge, where they could hear the music from within. Emily was relieved that she had on a jacket with a hood as they followed them inside, and a gentle, misty rain started to fall.

The place was crowded inside. The crew was carrying platters of delicious-smelling food upstairs, and the bar was always refilled with drinks. A woman was on stage, giving it her all while Kelly Rowland sang Ice.

Laurie yelled over the music, "Over there!"

They started to make their way across the packed floor after she gestured to the table close to the rear. Mark alerted the others of their coming before anyone else did.

"What took the two of you so long? Mark bobbled his head to the sound of the woman screaming over the microphone as they prepared to shut down the kitchen and open the dance floor downstairs.

"Traffic," Laurie uttered. She and Emily removed their jackets with a shrug and draped them on the rear of their seats. She waved down a server and said, "I need a drink."

The woman with the notepad asked, "What can I get you?" She looked amazing with her short haircut. Although she was asking Laurie the question, Emily was the center of her attention.

"I'd like a coke and rum. What is it that Emily wants?

Emily was giggling at the female performer. She heard her name and turned to face them. Glancing up, she saw the waitress grinning at her. "Well, just a sangria, please; go easy on the brandy."

The waitress took a moment to write down the drink's name and then walked away to make the order.

"Looks like someone is fond of them," Mark chuckled.

"Oh, you also looked at that." Bobby chimed in, "She was all up in her grill," and let out a big cackle.

Shaking her head, Gail reclined back in her chair. "You people are brutal. Do you not realize how embarrassing you are to her?

Karen agreed and defended her friend, saying, "Yeah, leave her alone."

It's awesome, ladies. This is the kind of treatment I'm used to. Emily smiled, "They're just angry that no one is taking a look at them. She immediately got up and took a few bucks out of her jacket pocket.

"What's your destination?" inquired Laurie.

She said, "To get my drink and sit at the bar," before vanishing into the throng.

Laurie frowned slightly as she watched her leave. She looked away from her to look at the others. "Have any of you noticed Emily's recent behavioural changes?"

Gail questioned, "What do you mean, different?" She leaned in to make sure she could hear Laurie pushing a strand of her long blonde hair behind her ear.

"You are aware. As if preoccupied or distracted," Laurie replied, giving them each a quick glance.

Mark remarked, "The only thing I've noticed is that she hasn't been going out with us lately." "I mean, her showing up tonight really shocked me."

"Me too," Bobby replied. She was upset about something when she last came out. It was never revealed by her. I believe she is bothered by something, but she is holding it all inside.

One of us should try to have a conversation with her about it. Karen said as much, but her eyes were fixed on Laurie.

"Yeah, I recognize that expression," Laurie sighed. "All right, tomorrow I'll ask her and see what she says. Still, I won't give up. All people have the right to keep their secrets.

"I relate to that," Gail remarked.

The announcer announced that the dance floor was open downstairs at that same moment. It appeared as though everyone got to their feet at once and began descending the steep stairs. The club hit Follow Me was blasting through the surround sound, and the music was bouncing louder than it had before. Men and women could be heard dancing below, exclaiming, "That's my song," throughout the lounge.

Emily was sipping her Sangria from a bar stool. It had just the right amount of fruit and orange juice, and it was cold and sweet. Although she wasn't a big drinker, she thought she could take this tiny mixture. She sat there, rocking back and forth while her body swayed to the tunes. She shut her eyes and allowed the well-known melody to relieve her tension.

She reached down to pick up her glass, feeling the want for another sip, only to find she was almost done.

"May I get you another one?"

Emily noticed a woman observing her from the left as she leaned against the bar. She had low, seductive eyes and was tall and fair-skinned. She looked mysterious tonight because she was rocking all black. Emily would often experience a flutter of intrigue, but she hasn't found somebody intriguing enough to go on a date in a while. Or perhaps you're not as into women as you once believed?

The woman took a step closer, but Emily never answered. She cried out to the barman, "Hey, let me get a light beer and another of whatever she's having."

After giving a nod, the barman hurried to mix Emily's drink. When he came back, he put Emily's Sangria in front of her and the woman's beer on a serviette. He helped the next customer and walked off after removing the empty glass and taking the money from her.

Emily responded, "Thank you," taking a sip from her straw. I don't need to be a jerk and rob myself of a complimentary beverage.

The woman reached for her beer and replied, "You're very welcome."

Emily remained silent. She did nothing but sit there and gaze into the mirror behind the bar. She watched as her pals got to their feet and headed downstairs to groove.

The woman said, "Are you going to make me ask?"

Emily grinned, refusing to look at her, knowing just what she wanted.

She joked, "Only if you want to know."

The woman looked down and smiled shyly. She raised her head, her glare a little more certain. "What is your name?"

"Emily Bawler," she said, maintaining her gaze fixed on the mirror.

"My name is Sherry Woods."

Julius was sitting next to me in class, and he looked like he was either really angry with me or really drunk, or perhaps both.

"Bro, it's unbelievable that you declined Therese Ford's kiss! He loudly whispered in my ear, "She's like the hottest girl on campus," but then he recoiled in agony at the sound of his own voice.

I attempted to clarify my position, but Julius remained uninterested in hearing me out or paying attention in class. He fell asleep the moment his head touched his desk.

Our instructor entered the room wearing a severe expression. He gave me a smile before glancing across at Julius and furrowing his brow. Apparently, Julius was not spared from our teacher's fury despite my star status.

"All right, new students, let's start the school year. I'll be teaching you statistics. Mr.Rosenblum is how I go by.

As soon as you hear your name called, please answer with a gift.

I knew it was time to put myself on autopilot when he started calling out names. I answered his call to my name with a "present" of my own.

I was about to assume that this would be another dull statistics lesson when I looked up and saw a bombshell, sandy-blonde woman rush through the door.

My statistics professor stated, "You're late, Miss Richards," in a serious manner.

I gave a shy smile. "Sir, I apologize. However, I arrived just in time because I arrived during attendance, didn't I? I replied in a kind way.

He shook his head and shot me a cold look.

Alright. Please take a seat.

I walked to the back row, bowing a little. I looked up as I hurriedly attempted to settle into my workstation and saw two bluish-green eyes staring at me.

My gaze met the man with whom I had just kissed intensely.

I smiled slightly at him, but he was motionless and ignored me.

He snapped out of his world when his companion nudged him. He turned away and glanced to the front.

I straightened my hair while trying to pay attention to what the professor was saying.

The truth was that I wouldn't say I liked statistics. That required statistics to be taken by all first-year students was a terrible idea. I found statistics to be very complex. I hated doing data analysis and interpretation. I rested my chin on my palm and sighed.

I detested my major in addition to statistics. Business was not what I wanted to study. I had no desire to take over my father's business. My goal was to become a fashion designer on my own. I dreamed of starting my own fashion brand and creating my own outfits. I had dreamed about it since I was a young child.

Daddy used to take me to all of the New York City fashion shows. Every time, we'd take a seat in the front row. When I looked at the celestial angels on the catwalk, he loved seeing my joy. However, Daddy used to often say, "Fashion shows are just for fun." You must have common sense. It is inevitable that just one fashion designer will succeed out of 10.

He threatened to stop talking to me if I declared fashion design as my major, so I wanted to fight. I had nothing else to do.

"You will have a companion for the duration of the semester. Working with someone helps incoming freshmen understand the content better, in my opinion," Mr.Rosenblum stated.

Oh no.

I rolled my eyes. I was not a fan of partners. There was always one person who had to do everything. Since I would be absolutely useless in this topic, all I hoped for was to be paired with a maths nerd.

"Green and Richards."

My name astonished me, and I didn't understand why all of my students were applauding. However, I later discovered that we were partnered. Our "kiss" seemed to be the talk of the university.

He was laughing with his friend, who was making fun of him when I turned to look at him.

I wasn't sure if I was supposed to be joyful or not. I was paired with the sexiest guy I've ever seen, but only a few seconds ago, I had hoped to be paired with a maths nerd.

The lecturer grinned at me as he invited us to go to our partners.

"Hello," he said.

I nibbled on my lip. My cheeks started to heat up, and my heartbeat started to quicken. Dear God. I was behaving like a girl of thirteen.

Hello. My name is Natalie Richards. I held out my hand, and he took it with pleasure. The second our hands met, I felt a current of electricity coursing through me.

Logan Green. I'll be counting on you, may I say that? He laughed. He had a sensual, deep voice.

With a wave of my palm, I laughed.

"Oh no, you wouldn't dare count on me if you don't want us to fail this goddamn class," I swatted his powerful shoulder in jest.

He shook his head and laughed.

"Are you prepared to begin our first task?" he asked, his glistening eyes meeting mine.

Since we would be spending the entire semester together,

Mr.Rosenblumwanted us to get to know our partners. To that aim, he gave us this goofy "secret code game" to solve in pairs. It was intended to promote teamwork. That sh*t was unbearable to me.

"Not really, but this class is looking better now that I have you as a partner," I mutely remarked, a cunning smile on my lips.

Up close, Logan looked much more gorgeous. Now that we were both clean, as opposed to that night when we were inebriated with drink and love, I could watch him.

He inquired, "Were you able to solve the second problem?" and that startled me out of my reverie. I chewed my lip while glancing at the flask.

I was unable to take the greatest temperature since I was preoccupied with his macho arms.

"Well, no." I gave a clumsy smile, blushing hot with shame.

I knew he would become enraged. He shook his head and grinned.

If you don't pay attention, Miss Natalie Richards, we'll have to spend hours in this classroom. Winking, he remarked calmly, "I know you have a class after this, not that I mind."

I batted my baby blues at Mr. Green and said, "Stop flirting with me, Mr. Green."

He muttered, "How can I when you are so beautiful?"

I nibbled on my lip.

Dear God. I believe my liking for numbers is growing.

You later," I said, turning to leave.

It was 5:30 p.m. when I got to Natalie's dorm. We had set a time of 6 p.m., but I didn't want to be late because I was so thrilled about the date. I, therefore, stood outside her dorm, impatient.

I knocked on her door at precisely 6:00 p.m. When she opened it, the most exquisite angel on the planet appeared before me. She accessorized with black high-waisted jeans, ankle boots, and a pink crop top. My body tensed as she took a stride in my direction. Even though I felt prepared for this, I was incredibly anxious. Her lips and eyes simultaneously smiled at me as she turned to face me.

"Hello!" I said. "You appear stunning," I continued, grinning like a young child.

"Mr. Green, where are you taking me? She joked, "Hopefully, you're giving me a night I won't soon forget," as she gave me a stomach punch.

"I suppose you'll have to wait to find out," I retorted slyly.

She smiled playfully in response to my response.

That jerk almost always gets away with it, too. No matter what, he's the only one who can always make me happy.

He took out his ostentatious popcorn popper and started our movie snacking.

"Reed." My voice trailed off when the kernels popped. Although I truly want to tell him about the business, I don't want him to focus more on work than having a good time with me.

Kar, what is it? The popcorn is almost done. Would you like to remove the M&Ms from the pantry?

"You're really filthy. Ew, popcorn and M&Ms. Although it seems like a snack from Frankenstein, it's actually quite tasty. It's one of the best ideas he's ever had, and the warmth from the popcorn causes the chocolate to melt somewhat. But since it's Reed, I like to make fun of him for it.

His whole demeanor seemed so carefree and content as he glanced over his shoulder at me. This is what I desire. I want this feeling to come over both of us as much as possible. Not just tonight, not only when we take off our clothing.

I would like a relationship with Reed Harrington IV. For true. Whoa, what a mess.

Hey, I think your poll results are fantastic. Does that imply that Maryanne will continue to make us appear adorable in public for the next month or so?

He gives an inattentive nod. Yes, most likely. It appears that everyone in Valentine's is rather happy that we are together.

"Regarding that—" I hesitate, not sure what to say.

"Yes," His hair becomes all rumpled over his forehead when his head raises at a slight angle. I want to muck things up and smooth it out at the same time.

"Rodney, are we really doing this? This thing between you and me?

He grabs me and tucks me up close to his body. "We're doing this, for sure. In fact, as often as I can get you to agree to it. With a murmur in my ear, he leans in my direction. "You know, I'm the one who enjoys our time together the most."

Oh, sh*t. He's gone and made me feel all warm and fuzzy again. "All right," I mumble.

"All right," he queries.

Just ok. Reed, it is really lovely to be with you. I pull myself closer to him. "I'm grateful that you are my boyfriend tonight."

He tenses up for a second, I sense. "Karisma, not only for tonight. I'm willing to be your boyfriend as long as you allow it.

I act as though considering his proposal. "Well, until I receive a better offer then, at least."

He snorts twice from an automobile's rear seat. They don't seem to present any better offers than that.

I dismiss him with a wave. "I've experienced better."

He nearly chokes on it. It was far too simple. He manages to bite out, "Jeffrey?" in a voice that is clearly offended.

"You know I'm not a woman to kiss and tell, Reed Harrington?" I saucily exit his kitchen. "Now that the snacks are here, let's get rid of the party attire. We'll practice this boyfriend-girlfriend stuff while watching your awful movie.

"My dear, I think giving up clothes is a part of the boyfriend-girlfriend dynamic."

"Yeah, and the movie and snuggling sessions. If this is going to be real, Kade, we have to do both.

"Kar, I'm prepared to give you anything you desire. That contains the most delectable movie munchies, an incredibly cozy couch, and engaging chat whenever you want to poke fun at the people in the movie or me.

That brings me to memory. We must have a conversation.

In a breath, I hear him hiss. Jerkface, hehe. I will undoubtedly cause him some discomfort occasionally if he is to be so sweet and affectionate towards me. We'll maintain harmony in our partnership in this way.

He gives a throat clear. "Is there a problem?"

The apparent fear in his voice makes me want to cry, but it takes a lot of self-discipline not to. He is far too naive to survive in this harsh, unforgiving world.

I slap him with my fingers. "Cosy attire, wealthy boy." Allow me to unzip myself. After that, we're going to have a discussion.

He pushes the bowl of M&Ms and popcorn into my hands and motions for me to move ahead of him. Indeed, I could grow accustomed to chasing after Reed Harrington IV. I've always enjoyed making fun of him, and now I have a whole new set of tools at my disposal.

Reed is not going to recognize what hit him.

I'm struggling mightily to maintain my composure, not to fuck KarismaTroudeau at this precise moment. I wanted to be inside her about thirty minutes ago, but I've done a fair and gentlemanly job of forcing her into the car twice on the way home, so 10 points for Gryffindor. I want to feel her close to me when she prays to God or, at the very least, mentions me in vain. Either might work, but I can't take any more of this.

She appears to be trying to make me feel lustful for her with everything she's done tonight. First of all, dressing up for a party like that should be against the law. Her wearing it all night was like waving a red cloak in front of a bull if the cape were her general sexiness, and the bull was actually my out-of-control horny boner-wielding ego. I had carefully bought it to suit her.

She then escalated the situation by scolding a group of horrible ladies who were attempting to disparage her. To me, nothing is more attractive than a confident lady. In fact, I think that's my favorite quality about Kar. She never apologizes for being authentically herself, even when it bothers other people. I adore that she is so confident in herself that she doesn't care what other people think of her. If only I was half as confident as that.

And then I nearly had a stroke during that mesmerizing dancing performance at the gala. I already found it offensive when guys would stare at her sleazy-eyed all night. However, as she arched her sensual curves towards me on that parquet floor, I could almost feel the lusty looks directed towards her. Guess who, nevertheless, gets to accompany her home tonight? Codger McCodgersons is correct. It's me. I was chosen by her.

I would assume that Kar had planned this entire evening in an attempt to be the woman who could tame me if she were any other woman. However, I am familiar with her. She is against my being subdued. She also wants neither my bank account nor my last name.

For the simple reason that we are meant to be together, Karisma Trudeau wants me. With us, even the sex is unmatched. Nobody I've ever met wants to play rough like me. She was meant to be mine, and most of the time, our compatibility has been flawless. Why, therefore, does she feel the need to talk about something other than "harder," "yes," and "just like that" at this moment?

She walks towards my bedroom as though she owns the area, and I have no choice but to follow the rhythm of her hips. To be honest, I like that. I can't stop thinking about how many evenings I've spent drinking at her bar, trying to avoid going to this ridiculous mausoleum of a house, yet when she's here, I genuinely feel content.

She walks across to my bedroom window and looks out into the night. Her curves are captured by the moonlight, which highlights her like a flower blooming at night.

I estimate that I have roughly twenty seconds before I go crazy and attack her out of pure lust.

"Kar," I whisper to myself. "What is happening, my love?" I move across to take her hand as gently as I can.

I touch her hand, and it feels clammy. How in the world? Did we not come here for nude moments or nasty talk?

When she finally turns to face me, her dark, wide eyes stare at me. "Reed, I have to tell you something very important."

I become icy. Oh my god. She is planning to end our relationship. We went out, and I could already tell that she had a terrible night and was about to break up with me.

I draw her up close to me and press her up against my body, pleading, "Please Kar." I inhaled sharply and desperately tried to think of a list of reasons why she ought to give me another go.

"Kade, your ridiculous tux is getting lipstick all over it. Your deposit won't ever be returned. Give me up, you stupid face. She pushes, not very gently, against me.

I'm trembling with fear. I was on the verge of devouring her like a savage, and now she's attempting to end our relationship. I swear, I'm such a fool. I try to control my freak out while running my fingers through my hair.

"Kar, I'm genuinely concerned about you. What's that? Was there anything I did incorrectly? On the final phrase, my voice practically breaks. Oh no. Really embarrassing. She's going to smell my fear and run for it, so I better get my head in the game here.

"Redden, I also received some very exciting news today." She gives me one of her gloomy stares and crosses her arms.

How come? Would you please tell me right away so I don't have a panic attack? I rap my foot frantically on the lux carpet, but it doesn't make a difference.

"I need your help with a new problem I have." Her mouth is dripping with sex as she speaks. Or is this scene being rewritten by my own hurting dick? I promise that when I'm around her in that dress, I can't think straight.

It seems like she wants to try something new and naughty in bed, so I must have misread something here. And while I wholeheartedly support it, why is she turning it into such a huge deal?

Hold on. Should she give anal a try?

There goes my cock once more, entering the group at the least advantageous moment.

Her eyes narrowed as if she could hear all of my dirty thoughts about her, loud and clear. "Kade, us." She makes a shooing-like motion with her hand flapping between us.

Does she continue to discuss Anaal? I'm completely perplexed.

"Kar, really. Could you please use small, dumb, guy-sized words? It's difficult for me to follow.

With a deep breath, she reaches up and strokes my jacket. "Tonight, I'm screwing everything up. My lipstick has gotten all over you.

"Kar, I want your lip gloss all over me, however, not on my clothing, but on my skin.

Her seductive lips remain firmly in place, but her eyes brighten with curiosity. "Red, I promised you earlier that we wouldn't use sex to solve every problem."

"But what should I fix? Whatever it is you're trying to tell me, I don't understand why we can't be talking while we're nude. At last, I can't resist pushing against her despite the distance. "Kar, we're best friends. Now, hurrah, we get to go through whatever is upsetting you while we're nude.

She withdraws from me once more, raising her arms in annoyance. But that's precisely what I'm saying. She gives a toss of her head, her long curtain of hair whirling about as it did on the night she had her head-banging, belly-dancing session at the bar. Observe? That's precisely what I mean when I say this.

I guess I've officially found myself stuck in an Abbott and Costello act with my ideal gal. This must be some kind of cosmic retribution for my childhood transgressions, most likely excessive masturbating.

I inhaled deeply. As soon as possible, I have to break us free from this pattern and get us naked. We can definitely figure out what's going on in her thoughts once our hormones have subsided a little.

"Kar." Her short outburst ends, and she finally looks me in the eye. "I'm attempting to determine my mistake

here, but you're not providing much assistance. I need a break, please.
She inhales deeply and gives a single nod.

"Cousin Itt is preferable to Pugsly." In order for him to see my face once again and for me to see his, I pushed my hair behind my ears. "Is there a deal here?" I extended my hand. He accepted it with both hands. We gave each other a shake.
"Agree," he murmured.
"Squeee!" Give thanks to the goddess. I didn't want to be forced to leave this course.
"I'm excited about it. The fact that one set of paintings can get me two grades? It makes perfect sense. Is my roommate being joked about? What is your current schedule like?
After looking over our calendars, Matt and I discovered that there were

multiple overlapping blocks of the week when we weren't in class. Matt seems to be as excited about this collaboration as I was. I was shocked at how at ease I felt with him, even though our socioeconomic statuses couldn't be more different.

"So, is there anything you need me to do between now and Monday?" he said.

"Just make sure you register for the class tomorrow, please, please, please."

Chapter Six: Matthew

In order to have one day—well, one morning and early afternoon—where I wasn't required to be anywhere for someone, I purposefully scheduled no classes for Friday. It was a weekend, in my opinion. I had no remorse about sleeping in, studying, painting, or playing video games. My Sunday was Friday, and I never made plans to do anything until 3 p.m., when my mother would come to get me and take me back to the farm.

Never, ever, until I shook hands with Abbie last night and said I would sign up for today's Neuroscience 201 session, first of all.

When you stay up till three in the morning, lunch comes first. All I had to do was go to the college registration website, click a few links, transfer money for the course cost, and call it done, so I didn't worry. However, I received a warning from the system saying that it was busy and to "try again in a few minutes." I made multiple unsuccessful attempts before deciding at two o'clock that I should go in person to the Registrar's Office to complete the process.

I knew I wasn't the only student who thought it, given the number of other students who were present—at least twenty. I was led directly into the office by a security guard when I crossed the line. Triumph!

The admin person questioned, "Dropping or registering?"

"I'm registering," I said as I took my wallet out of my rear pocket.

He motioned for me to store it. Not yet necessary for that. We're handling course dropouts first, and after we've finished them, we'll give you a call to allow you to enroll in another course.

"When do you think that will happen? Say, within the next hour or half an hour? At three, I have a ride coming up.

He produced an expression that said, "Don't be stupid," and "I'm sorry," so perfectly. I'd made several attempts to paint that look, but I still hadn't discovered the secret. The eyes?the oral cavity? Head? His countenance altered as he spoke, just as I was going to say, "Don't move," as I reached for my phone to take a picture.

"My friend, you have seven or eight o'clock to go tonight. Your weekend plans will, I'm afraid, have to wait until tomorrow.

"Will there also be an online registration back up?"

Not in a million years. Last night, it was compromised. With students going by the titles of Cat Hacker, Dog Puker, Goat Regurgitator, and so on, every course is now fully enrolled. Even in courses, we have to manually remove them in order to see where seats remain.

When I told my dad I wouldn't be coming home tonight, I imagined his reaction. It was another statement of frustration and disappointment that I hadn't been able to depict well.

"Please put your name and phone number here. Stay near to campus; we'll call you fifteen minutes before we need you here, the registrar dude stated.

"Combining seven and eight?"

"Ish."

Fantastic. I nodded and smiled at the person, then went to my studio to try to catch the expression on his face while it was still fresh in my mind. On the way, I gave Mom a call.

"Hi, my love. Are you prepared for the weekend?

"Hey, Mom."About that. I'm unable to attend. I had to enroll in a course because the school's course registration system was compromised. To do everything in person, I have to be here by seven or eight this evening.

She said, "Your dad is going to be disappointed."

"I am aware. Are you going to tell him? Would you please, Mom?

"Um."

"Come get me early tomorrow morning." I asked, feeling more comfortable offering the advice even though I knew the response.

When did the Mom Bus start running on weekends? I have everything I need to cook lasagna tomorrow, so it's too bad—your loss. Her smile was audible in her voice. "Honey, I'll see you over the weekend. About your dad, don't worry. He'll enlist the assistance of a nearby child. Just be aware that your portion of the inheritance will be used to pay them.
"Mom, you are loved. Apologies. And I appreciate your understanding.
I also adore you, my dear. Enjoy your enjoyable weekend.
I started a new sketch paper sheet at my studio, placed it on the easel, and scribbled "Don't be stupid" and "I'm sorry" at the top. I then began to draw faces.
I had drawn and painted a lot of expressions in an hour, but none of them quite matched my intended look. It was my version of the Mona Lisa of expressions, elusive and uncapturable.

My phone pinging with a text message was a much-needed diversion.

Abbie: Are you game?

Me: Just about. Have you learned of the hack?

Abbie: Indeed. Absurd.

Abbie: How are you doing?

Me: the studio

Abbie: I own the EEG equipment. Shall I bring it over?

Me: of course

After five minutes, the door was knocked on.

"Enter now!" I made a call.

Leaning over the door, Abbie looked in. Or rather, a voice shouting unintelligible nonsense materialized around the corner, accompanied by a head of long black hair. "Dihdium d'oh d'yehd'ya."

I chuckled. It's great to see you again, Cousin Itt. You say donuts? Please, I would really like one.

Setting down my brush, I approached her. I felt a small thrill of excitement when she flipped her hair away from her face and smiled.

Tell me about the registration mess, please. She inquired, giving me a kind tap on the shoulder as she went by, "You can still get into the class, right?" and proceeded to the area where my easel was placed. Yes, I did feel quite comfortable about our arrangement.

I told her everything, even the fact that I had to spend the weekend on campus.

"When was the last weekend you spent here?" She was crouching on the floor, plugging a little machine the size of a suitcase into a power socket, when she looked up.

"The school year kickofflobster bake. And when it rolls around again, I have a feeling Dad is going to tell me I've already spent my holiday weekend.

She shot me a sardonic smirk, and my dick began to show interest in taking a look at my plumpelicious lab partner—for the second time in five minutes.

I turned away and grabbed up my brush once again, planning to keep adjusting the makeup on my face. But all I wanted to work on was drawing Abbie because that was the only form I could think of. I straightened, pulling up my suddenly too-tight boxer underwear, and realized it was the only shape I wanted to sketch.

I'd never responded like this when I imagined a naked woman. Hell, I'd never responded like this when a nude woman sat in front of me. I found those bodies to be just as sensual as a bowl of avocados. Or lifeless frogs.

She added, "I was thinking maybe we could do a quickie with the equipment since you're stuck here and, I assume, don't have plans, and I don't have plans either."

She didn't just say that, oh my goodness. She looked like an anime character with her eyes wide open, gasping as she approached me while clutching what appeared to be a swimming cap of torment. I hoped it was a response to my own look of astonishment or to recognizing what she'd said. I hoped she hadn't noticed the gun in my camouflage shorts that appeared out of nowhere.

In her nightmares, Bonnie kept hearing the same kiss. Not the initial kiss she'd planned to give him to get Mara off her back, the hit-and-run kind. No. That second kiss, the one that melted over you like butter, was what had kept her up the entire night. That and the recollection of his scent, which delightedly danced with her senses and included spices and woods.

Going to the department shop and selecting a new fragrance for Marcus was one of her favorite things to do for him.

In a desperate attempt to avoid the memories and the emotions it evoked, Bonnie pushed back the covers. She and Mara shared a pitch-black chamber, with hints of dawn peeking around the edges of the drapes. Bonnie padded to the open space by the windows, being careful not to wake her. Apart from the sound of the motel air conditioner, everything was silent. Bonnie stretched her arms and neck, breathing in and out deliberately as she pushed her attention to focus on the music and then the empty serenity surrounding it. She reached automatically for the yoga regimen that had helped her maintain her sanity after her husband's death and helped her preserve what little of their once-ideal two-parent life for their three children.

At first, she had written off yoga as new-age nonsense. The poses were challenging, though, and she'd never been one to back down from a challenge, so she persevered. Just as adjusting to life without Marcus had gotten easier, so too had the poses become less work for her. Day by day, breath by breath.

She added the leg lift—hold, deep breath in, exhale, release—and pushed back into downward dog halfway through the routine. She then stretched her left leg through her arms into a forward lunge. The end of her braid swept across her cheek in a manner reminiscent of how his fingertips had caressed her skin in the elevator the night before.

She withdrew from him at that point. She became aware that a stranger's touch had awakened long-slumbering limbs in her by sending shockwaves of yearning through her. She had believed that she had buried all of her feelings and desires with Marcus, but now they were resurfacing and betraying her like cold, hard coals.

Betraying him.

A sudden sob lodged in the back of Bonnie's throat, causing her to miss her next move and collapse onto her knees. The scream startled Mara, causing Bonnie to quickly get up and run to the bathroom in hopes that the sound of her sobbing would be drowned out by the shower's spray.

Mara had already turned over when Bonnie reappeared, dressed, her garments packed up. She let out a moan and asked for water and two painkillers.

Bonnie delivered them to her. "Do you regret drinking that last champagne glass?"

"I regret the first because my head hurts so much." Reaching for the water, Mara

sat up. "A parcel was left for you while you were taking a shower. Jenson or Jason?Claimed to be the hotel's night manager.
"What's that?"
She murmured, "I dunno," while holding a mouthful of tablets. She defeated them. "Someone left it for you at the front desk, according to the manager."
The Windermere emblem was etched in the corner of the white box that stood outside their door. Mara saw Bonnie pry open the seal. The shoe she had lost the previous evening was nestled in soft tissue paper. Beside it was a message tucked in.
"Is this from him, please?" Excitement permeated Mara's speech.
"No duh," chuckled Bonnie. It was him that forced me to let it go.
"Yes, he did," Mara laughed. "What does it say?"

Before reading aloud, Bonnie quickly examined the exact lettering to make sure there was nothing that would make her look even more foolish. "Good morning, the Fairy Tale. I apologize for how last night ended, and I would love to have coffee with you today to make things right. Across the street is a fantastic store. I'll wait for you there until nine o'clock.

Bonnie laughed at the last line of the note.

With her hangover forgotten, Mara leaped across the bed and reached for the message. Go through the remainder. Was his name signed by him?

Bonnie responded, "No," after it was safely out of her reach. Just now, he added a P.S. Bonnie recited the passage once more to himself.

Cinderella trusted Prince Charming despite the fact that he was a stranger.

Whatever. I will ultimately learn. Mara rolled her eyes and looked at the time. "Are you heading there? If so, you should move quickly. It's beyond eight already.

She was tormented by her feelings from this morning. "I'm not sure if I should,"

"Go!" With a stumble, Mara got out of bed and went to get Bonnie's bag off the dresser. She pulled Bonnie in the direction of the door after forcing it into her hands. You can use it as practice for approaching males again if nothing else. Additionally, you'll be able to move past that awful first date experience.

"There isn't a date." Bonnie retreated. And why do you believe it will be so awful?

"No, I don't. I simply want to say, ugh! Never mind. Get yourself some coffee. Enjoy yourself. I'll pack everything and take a shower. Mara, never one to pass up an opportunity, reached for the note one final time. "Allow me to pack that in your suitcase."

"Good attempt." Bonnie laughed as she strolled down the hallway, holding the piece of paper to her chest. "I'll store it in my bag for protection."

Bonnie moved aside to make room for the group of patrons entering Magic Beans behind her. She stopped and breathed in the rich, dark aroma of freshly made coffee while her eyes adjusted to the low light. Delectable.

The posh store had a charming personality. Scattered across a large expanse of stained concrete are groups of seats and leather couches that appear to be pleasant. The distant wall of bare brick was covered in deep green ivy, while above her, tiny lights shimmered against the charcoal ceiling like stars in the night sky.

She caught a glimpse of a man getting up from one of the couches. She waved back and, thinkinglessly, smiled as he waved. How different from herself.

He wore pants and a gray button-down today, dressing more casually. The curl showed through in his thick dark hair, which seemed more finger-raked this morning. He seemed to be even more incredibly attractive than he was the night before.

"Good morning," he began in a voice that matched the mood of the room—rich and ominous. Delightfully captivating. "I started to believe you wouldn't be coming,"

She wasn't, it dawned on her abruptly, but after reading the remainder of his note, his P.S. made her reconsider. I was in the shower when the delivery arrived, and Mara neglected to notify me about it. I appreciate you sending back my shoes.

"I express my gratitude for granting me another opportunity," he added, extending his hand. "Wilkerson Chuck."

"Sullivan, Bonnie." Her hand felt little in his, yet not in a menacing way, but secure and comforting. And just like the previous time, that damned thrill ran down her limbs. "I'm glad to have met you."

And we are no longer strangers. Bonnie. She felt a chill run down her spine as he softened his voice and said her name. That deadly smile of his reappeared. "We had better line up. On Sundays, things get a little crazy around here.

The line moved swiftly, and throughout their wait, they talked about the several beverage selections featured on the menu board. Bonnie decided on a double espresso in the end. Chuck placed the same order.

As Bonnie cast glancing looks at him, she noted the way his eyebrow lifted. "You appear taken aback. Were you anticipating that I would order some frothy, caramel-dripping mocha latte? She wrote him what she imagined was a flirtatious message, smiling at the way he half-shrugged in response. "It's my order for the afternoon."

His warm, wonderful laugh tickled all the right spots in her ears. The barista brought her a cup, which she accepted. "What am I supposed to say? I spend all day with children. Only oxygen is more potent than caffeine.

"Identical." Chuck thanked the cashier and put his wallet away, still grinning. They remained silent till they took a seat at a table that was hidden in a peaceful corner.

Putting forth the first question that was sure to come, she questioned, "So, what do you do that requires all that caffeine?"

"I recently moved to a new town to support my sister on a project. And cover for her as a substitute babysitter when necessary. She is going through a protracted divorce and holds a prominent position.

"Aww." From the sound of it, prolonged swiftly turned into messy, and that was never good, especially with kids. Bonnie sent her her condolences.

"So, what do you do for a living that involves spending all day with children?"

"By day, I teach English in high school." Mom at night.

Nothing was revealed by his look. "Simple superhero stuff."

"That or something similar."

"How big of a kid are you?

Bonnie inhaled deeply. This is definitely what would entice a new guy to cut and run if anything. "Three."

"Triple?"

Her shoulders tensed, and there was a challenge in the way she met his stare. Indeed, three. Two daughters and a boy.The twins.

She most likely believed that the news alone ought to frighten him. And it did—in a positive sense. She truly was a superhero. Regardless of the situation that made her a single mother, she had endured enough to not tolerate any games.

Raising his cup, he took a sip and drew closer. Tell me about them, please. What interests them?

She averted her gaze and fidgeted with the napkin next to her. "You didn't ask me to coffee to discuss my kids," I said.

She was about to escape, instinct telling him, so he decided to take a chance and covered her hand with his. He grinned when she looked up. "Bonnie, I wanted to get to know you, which is why I invited you. You are a part of your children. Squeezing her fingers, he released them. It's likely that you find it simpler to talk about your children than yourself if you're anything like my sisters. Correct?

Her shoulders loosened a little, but that guarded gaze persisted. "Siblings? What number do you have?

Plus, three brothers make two. Everyone older than I am.

"So you're the family's baby? I guess it's spoiled rotten.

"It's not my fault that I'm everyone's favorite."

Her eyes were no longer tightly strained. He was a secure subject. Alright. He took out his phone and pointed to all of the siblings, their spouses, and kids as he looked through a number of photos from his niece's graduation ceremony.

Chuck, at Bonnie's request, went back in time to his favorite photo of the evening, which showed him with all of his nieces and nephews; the majority of them were crammed onto his back or in his lap.

"Look—my favorite uncle."

When her fingertips contacted him while she picked up the phone, he experienced that surge of excitement once more. She did, too, judging by the way her eyes shot up to meet his.

She looked back at the phone, her lips moving as she counted faces in silence.

Thirteen, and one more is on the way.

Bonnie, I'm not afraid of kids because I come from a large family.

Her mouth curved full of lips. "Spoken like a guy who has never gone through a Lego minefield at two in the morning barefoot."

Indeed. However, I did have some experience because I dressed up as a clown for Layla's birthday last year.

"Wow, that sounds quite harsh." She crossed her arms and leaned back, laughing.

"Let me tell you something, girls the age of five do not enjoy clowns."

"No, not typically.Bethie didn't enjoy them till she was seven years old. Grace didn't do that. A dimple showed through her kind smile. "Until you try to organize a birthday party for twins who are seven years old and have abruptly decided they don't want to wear the same clothes or have the same interests, you have no idea how difficult it can be." However, they continue to do so. They simply go through this strange phase while they look for freedom. What's worse is that even they are unable to maintain track of who likes what. For weeks, they had us circling around in circles in an attempt to come up with something.

She fidgeted once more as her laughter faded, and she tugged at her sleeve. Her fingers finally stopped moving as the recollection took over.

After giving her room, he enquired, "So what did you end up doing?"

A traveling circus. Marcus recommended it to make sure we covered all the bases.

"Is Marcus your son?"

"My late husband—my husband." There was a strain in her voice. She grabbed her phone and hurriedly flipped through an album till she came to a picture.

He was met with five beaming faces in return. A boy was hoisting a fake barbell aloft, and two girls, one costumed like an acrobat and the other like a lion tamer, stood on either side of him. The females pointed to his biceps, hammering home an expression of shock. Bonnie was standing behind them, wrapped around her ringmaster's arm like a circus monkey.

"Your family is stunning. Attractive man.

"Many thanks. He was. I believe Justin resembles him quite a bit. She grabbed the phone, swiping the picture to reveal another child to him. "Please pardon all of the goofy faces. Back then, we were a bunch of goofs.

"And right now?"

"The children are still there. I make an effort for them. Simply put, it's different.

"May I inquire as to what transpired?"

When she gave him the phone this time, he was only looking up at one face. Her spouse, in his uniform, looked solemn.

One evening, Marcus took on an additional shift and while on patrol, Her eyes averted. "He always hurried into things."

His wind was taken away by those final words. Would she run if he told her he was a firefighter? "I'm so—" says Bonnie.

"Avoid. Please. Her fingers trembled as she pushed a strand of dark hair behind her ear. "The only reason I'm telling you is to make sure you comprehend what happened last night. Looking back, I suppose I may have had too much champagne, too, as my buddy Mara had consumed far too much of it. Well, she's been pressuring me to go back into the dating game because she worries that I haven't moved on from Marcus.

"Do you?"

Indeed. No, really, but I wanted Mara to think that I had. Her brow furrowed in confusion. "But at the time, I didn't think I had."

Although he found it difficult to grasp her reasoning, the truth was evident in her eyes and in the fact that she was present with him. Long after they've finished their coffee, they're still talking to him. A sense of hope sprang in him. "Until last night, you didn't think you were over him?"

Leaning forward, she said, "It was a foolish impulse." Really, it's a dare. A little kiss to let her go off my back. That was the only thing this was ever meant to be.

Then I gave you a kiss. And it also felt like you."

"It? No. Her side-swept hair flew into her eyes with a strong headshake. "I still don't know what I felt like."

"Nevertheless, you sensed something," he urged.

"It was most likely just the champagne buzz."

Why don't we try something out?

"I'm not going to kiss you again." Her gaze grew wide as she took in the packed room. "I don't usually make out in public, regardless of the impression I must have given you last night."

I was very tempted to go out on a make-out session with her. "No, not this time for a kiss."

"All right," she shook her head. "I'm not going to do anything more than give you a kiss just yet."

He forced a smile from his lips. "I like the way you said yet."

Her eyebrow furrowed. "What?"

"You said yet. Like you're considering more at some point." He sat back with a grin, seeing a most delicious shade of pink flush her cheeks. "I was going to suggest something like a trial run."

"Trial run? You sound like a science nerd."

He shrugged, not trying to refute it because he was one. "It'll be a chance for you to see if you're ready and a chance for us to get to know each other. Ten dates—"

"Ten. Definitely not. Two maybe—but only if this counts as one of the dates."

"Oh, so we're bargaining now? Five, final offer." He leaned closer, challenging. "And coffee is neutral. It never counts as a date, which is why I proposed it."

"Well, this coffee counts, and three is my final offer."

"Done." He stretched out his hand, and happily, she shook it before she pondered anything that would change her mind. "But, the coffee doesn't count."

I'm simply heading to the store to grab lunch for the two of us. I'm shocked to see Nana Lily shouting from 1944.

Alright, My voice sounds strained as I yell, overcome with guilt at almost being caught reading these love letters. The glass inserts rattle as the front door slams shut.

I get up and extend. If these letters were Grammy's secrets, maybe I shouldn't be reading them. I plan to continue working as I sit down, but the letters are calling to me. I am powerless to resist.

I exhale, then carry the box, picture, and letters I've read to my bed. I drop to the ground and rest my back on the bed's leg. Although sleeping on the duvet might be more comfortable, it would be uncomfortable to read a love letter to Grammy while lying on my great-grandparents' bed.

I lay everything out on the floor next to me so I could see the picture while I read, and then I reached in to get the next letter. The date on it is September 10, 1944.

My sweetheart, English Rose, your shrewdness and fast thinking continue to amaze me. How fortunate it was that the Major's vehicle broke down en route to his meeting in London, and how astute you were to volunteer to give him a lift back. Naturally, curfew meant that you had to remain overnight.

We had dinner at the neighborhood pub, which was a great treat. You were brave to meet my friends at the bar afterward. The most memorable part, though, was when we were about to return to the barracks. The only time we spent the entire evening together was for that minute or two when I pulled you back behind the steps.

Your blue eyes captivated me, and your lips formed a small smile that appears when you're thinking of positive ideas.

Even though I knew better, I couldn't help myself. I reached down and put my lips to yours. I just wanted to steal a quick kiss, but I was gone when you put your arms around me and kissed me again.

I slid my hands over the curves of your back, my heart racing so fast I thought I might have a heart attack.

I'm sorry, but I felt like embracing you and bringing you upstairs. Luckily, the barman cut us off. I apologize if I embarrassed you in any way; as I said my goodbyes, your cheeks turned red.

I'm not sorry, even though I should be, for taking advantage of you. The kiss left a lasting impression.

I have just one month left before my next trip to London.

Until then, Marlon, yours.

Whoa, it seems like Grammy kissed a different man, and it was a really passionate and heated kiss.

The idea is making my head spin. Grammy was getting old by the time I started thinking about kissing boys. She was elderly, but she was still gorgeous, and it was obvious that she had been quite the sight in her younger years. It was shocking to discover that she had kissed a GI in a dimly lit hallway.

My hand is going for the next letter, an updated one, even as these ideas race through my mind.

I hope this reaches you before my anticipated leaving date, my sweet English Rose, and that you don't have to wait at the station wondering if I've abandoned you. Although he is unsure if he will be able to visit your office this week, my friend assures me that he will forward it to someone who can deliver it to you.

Something is moving us. For obvious reasons, I can't tell you where, but whoever delivers this should be able to tell you roughly where it is.

I won't be able to visit London, but my leave date remains the same. I'll write as soon as I can.

Marlon, you

Marlon's worry over the error shows through in the letter. It could not have been simple to organize to catch up and then had to make last-minute planned changes when there was a war going on. It wasn't like he could send a little text, really.

There are four more letters in the packet to read, so I'm very confident they got together again. I turned to the next one, November 28, 1944, and continued reading.

My lovely and astute Rose

Since we have been working long shifts, I haven't had time to write. You have to consider me to be a cad, as you English people say. You probably think that because I achieved what I desired, I've abandoned you. Maybe I haven't gotten what I want yet, but I'm not that kind of man. That is a jest.

Sweetheart Rose, When you finally showed up in Portsmouth, I was blown away. My eyes were seeing things my brain was not able to grasp, and all I wanted to do was stand there and take it all in.

Thankfully, you don't just have the looks—you also have the brains—and you grabbed my arm to show me where the tea house was. You filled in the silence as I stood there silently, amazed at my good fortune.

I volunteered to walk you back to the army base, where guests usually stay, as the sun started to drop. Then you shocked me by telling me that the army believed you were staying with relatives and that I had to bring you back to my accommodations or else you would have to spend the night on the streets.

You weren't joking, despite what I assumed. I thought I would burst into tears of excitement when you told me you loved me and that life was too uncertain to put things off. That was, without a doubt, the greatest night of my life.

I went to see my commanding officer today and requested permission to get married to you because only then will I be able to have what I really want, which is a future together.

I'm hoping to get permission to ask you the question I've been dying to ask before I go on Christmas break.

Marlon, your ever-loving

I'm hooked on Grammy Rose's letters right now. She had an extramarital affair with a US soldier. I'm not a prude, and I think well of her, but in the past...I suppose a lot of girls were doing it and going about their lives as if tomorrow never came. And a tonne of them were also falling for GIs. As a school project, I once completed a family tree and came across almost 6,000 marriages between British women and American soldiers. Continue.

Grammy!
My mouth became parched. Well, maybe don't go, Grammy. Perhaps poor Grammy—I know she had loved Marlon—but she didn't marry him.
A few days after Nana Lily's birth, she and Grandpa Frank traveled to Australia. She enjoyed sharing tales of how challenging it was to cross the sea while traveling with a small child and a new spouse.
My fingers linger over the final three characters. Is it truly my desire to know what went wrong? Can I survive in the

dark? The next letter is dated February 1, 1945, and is frankmarked.

Sweet Rose, my darling

I'm happy that we can now write again. It seems so impersonal to talk to you on the phone. Most of the time, I can scarcely hear you, and it's not very private because so many others are waiting to use the same phone. After all, they've crossed the borders. Therefore, it doesn't really matter anymore, and something significant must be on the horizon.

It seems like a fairy tale when I look back on it, and I can hardly believe you pulled it off. A cottage in the New Forest for the weekend. It was a pure delight to wake up in the morning to find you still asleep, your golden curls a halo around your face, cooking meals together, and taking leisurely strolls through the forest. It felt like all of this had vanished, and we were just a regular couple spending our evenings together in front of a crackling fire.

Yes, you are correct that life is too short to be concerned with tradition, but what can I say? You have a thing for traditional men. After everything is completed, I will take you home and present you to my family as my wife. I will obtain permission to marry you.

When we get together, I expect to share some wonderful news. We will be able to meet shortly.

A person's first kiss leaves a lasting impression. However, kissing can appear like a complicated act to some people, particularly if you've never tried it. In several screenplays, poetry, novels, and even songs, kissing has been immortalized. But how can you really make that first kiss last as long as it should? Reading this ebook can be quite beneficial if you are among the many people who haven't tried it yet but are itching to kiss that particular someone. You'll discover how to arrange the ideal scenario, project confidence, and, of course, execute all the technical tasks flawlessly (without appearing at all technical).

Your first kiss won't be insignificant or, worse, an embarrassing experience you'd rather forget. It will be a step towards getting to know that particular someone you truly appreciate on a more personal level. This is too crucial a moment to let slip by unprepared. A flawless kiss has the power to leave a lasting impression and will probably inspire many more in the future. A less-than-ideal kiss, however, can indicate that your developing romantic relationship is about to terminate.

© 2014 LCPublifish LLC Copyright - All rights reserved.

The purpose of this document is to give accurate and trustworthy information on the subject and problem discussed. The publication is marketed under the false impression that the publisher is exempt from providing officially authorized, qualified, or accounting services. A qualified practitioner should be consulted if legal or professional counsel is required.

- From a Declaration of Principles that both a Committee of Publishers and Associations and an American Bar

Association Committee recognized and approved in equal measure.

No portion of this text may be copied, reproduced, or transmitted in any form or by any electronic or hard copy means. It is highly forbidden to record this publication, and storing it longer than necessary without the publisher's explicit consent is also illegal. All rights reserved.

The material presented here is claimed to be accurate and consistent, with the caveat that the receiving reader bears sole and complete responsibility for any liability resulting from misuse or inattention while using any of the policies, procedures, or instructions included. The publisher shall not be subject to any legal liability or blame for any damages, compensation, or financial loss resulting from the information contained in this publication, whether caused directly or indirectly.

All copyrights not owned by the publisher belong to their respective authors.

This information is general in nature and is provided only for informational reasons. The information is being presented without any kind of warranty or obligation.

The trademarks are used without authorization, and the trademark owners have neither supported nor granted permission for the trademark to be published. The brands and trademarks used in this book are held by their respective owners and are merely used for clarification; they are not associated with this work.

You may have laughed at the idea of giving someone a passionate kiss when you were younger. Perhaps you've wondered, "Why is kissing such a big deal?" The act of sharing your first kiss will likely signal the beginning of a blossoming romance and the physical aspect of attraction.

A physical connection officially begins—or, regrettably, occasionally ends—with the first kiss. It will enable you to ascertain whether there is chemistry or a spark between the two of you. It also decides whether or not there will be a sexual climax. Consider this first kiss generally successful if you are both delighted to kiss each other and you have bodily or sexual excitement at that same instant.

But there are other times when one of you isn't prepared for what's about to happen. This is why the whole first kiss experience could end in a collapse. This is one of those times in your life when there are a lot of options. You never know what might occur if you don't just take the chance. Even while it could feel like jumping off a cliff, if you're ready, you can take some of the uncertainty back in control. If you know what you're going to do and how to go about it, the odds will be in your favor.

Chapter 2: Selecting the Appropriate Time

One of the most unforgettable moments of your life will be your first kiss. Therefore, to make sure that everything goes as planned, you might need to take the initiative to organize the situation in a way that increases the likelihood that it will be ideal.

Look and smell nice.

When someone appears careless, nobody wants to kiss them. This will undoubtedly spoil the occasion. When preparing for your first flawless kiss, appearance and scent play a big role. It won't be enough to just brush your teeth and change your pants every day. It is not enough for you to do it. It's imperative that you seem confident and respectful of both yourself and the person you intend to pucker up with.

Appear Clean and Invigorated

After taking a long shower, wash your face with a cleanser to remove any leftover oil or debris. Make sure you use a cleanser or exfoliant designed for oily skin if you have really oily skin. Someone's eyes will be just millimeters away, so you don't want your face to appear overly oily. Make sure all of your toenails and fingernails have been properly clipped by looking under them.

Put on an impressive look.

Choosing the appropriate attire is also crucial. Put on something that makes you feel confident and at ease at the same time. Make sure your outfit is appropriate for the evening or the occasion if you are heading out on a formal or romantic date. In order to prevent one of you from showing up too or too little dressed, make sure your date is aware of the expected outfit beforehand. It's a good idea to confirm that you both understand each other.

Plan ahead so that your favorite clothing isn't in the laundry basket on the day of your date; your clothes should smell and look good. Verify that there are no loose threads or missing buttons. Make sure your shoes and outfits complement each other by testing out the ensemble's color coordination. This will help you look amazing overall and entice your date to spend more time with you.

It Matters What Your Hair Does

There is nothing unusual or elaborate that you need to do if your hair looks well-maintained. However, if your regular appearance is a little boring, this would be a good opportunity to experiment or seek some assistance. Naturally, begin with a thorough shampoo in the shower. However, if you'd like, you can also get a professional haircut at a nearby salon or barbershop. You do want your date to recognize you, so there's no need to make a big alteration, but even a small improvement can help.

brand-new, flawless teeth

It is a fact that you should wash your teeth at least twice a day as part of your regimen. But there's more you need to do than that to get ready for an unforgettable first kiss. Not just first thing in the morning and just before bed, but right at the kiss itself, you'll need to breathe clean air. What would happen if you had a kiss during the day? A less-than-fresh lips or bad breath can put people off.

In addition to brushing your teeth as usual, make sure to floss and swish mouthwash around your mouth. Moreover, abstain from consuming any strong or smelly food right before your intended kiss. Not a lot of garlic, onion, or seafood.

Take chapstick or something comparable for the hour before the kiss. Put it in your pocket before you leave the house, and when the time comes, put some on. This can assist your spouse in feeling more at ease and comfortable kissing you during the time you have been waiting for—your first kiss!

Obtain His/Her Alone Time for Yourself

You probably want to make the most of your first kiss. You have to be able to get him/her anywhere by yourself as a result. You would think it would be a little strange to share your first kiss with friends or relatives. You most definitely don't want to look foolish in front of people, nor do you want anyone to sabotage the occasion. Additionally, if you do this in front of someone you are interested in, they might think you are just bragging. You must create a quiet, private atmosphere where you can be by yourself. We'll go over some excellent pointers for getting him or her to step out of the throng.

Most of the time, you'll be able to tell when it's appropriate to leave him/her alone. It is imperative that your spouse feels at ease with this as well. Examine the person's eyes to determine whether they seem content and at ease enough to spend time alone with you. After putting your hands in theirs, slowly step back from the throng. The sense of intimacy you are attempting to convey will be communicated through this type of physical touch. Ask your friends whether it's okay if you spend time together alone. This is probably going to work since everyone enjoys having their entire attention directed towards them. You can even arrange to ask that individual out on a date in advance if you'd want to avoid having to make the decision on the spur of the moment. In this manner, you are assured of spending time together alone before you even begin.

Now, to Establish the Tone

Make sure you are in a romantic environment or somewhere really noteworthy or exceptional. This is crucial, so be sure you've considered and made all the essential arrangements. Having a movie date at home, having an outdoor picnic in a peaceful park, or visiting an abandoned location are some of the best scenarios. Why not try a location with a beautiful view of the setting sun or spend a romantic evening on the beach as the stars come out?

It is not a good idea to turn off the lights during your first kiss if you are indoors. Don't completely turn them off, but feel free to dim them. You won't be able to hide your anxiety by doing this, and you might even make a mistake or look awkward. Those who are new to kissing in the dark aren't quite ready for the moment. It might just make matters more challenging. You won't ever get to witness your partner's reaction to the kiss, either! It would be best if you left the lights on for the time being and saved your plans to kiss in a dark area for when you're more experienced and confident in your kissing abilities.

Examine the Subtext

Determine whether your spouse is excited to kiss you and whether this is something they have done previously. However, remember that neither of you can be bashful. You might just need to take a deep breath, muster some confidence, and try it—one of you has to initiate the move first.

Here are several indicators that the person you like is interested in you to assist you in your search for them.

When speaking with you, the individual seems at ease and joyful, and occasionally, they even try to get your attention.

Whenever you gaze in their direction, you notice that they are making brief glances in your direction.

When you are conversing with someone, he or she bites their lips, blushes, and grins a lot.

The individual tries to establish physical touch with you. In addition, you might notice that while you are near each other, their breathing becomes labored.

1. They are pursuing her.

As she entered the shower, thirty-year-old Fernanda exclaimed, "Why me?" "No entiendo."

Why did the FBI think she was a murderer? Why were men posted here in Arkansas to keep an eye on the cabin? Why did they always follow her around?

And what about the others—the Peruvian shaman, the Indian holy man—why had they said that she was destined to be sacrificed from birth? Not for her benefit but rather for the benefit of humanity. They say she had to pass away in order for the earth to continue turning.

"No entiendo!"

How did she end up involved in this? How was she going to escape?

She cleaned her face. Feeling nice, her breasts were no longer tightly bound. She knelt and used the estropajo to wash her legs. She recalled seeing people taking baths in the Ganges in India, their brown skin sudsing up waist-deep in the green river. India, the land of terrible fantasies for her.is the location where the insanity started.

How did she end up involved in this? How was she going to get away?

And her dreams were much worse at night. Even worse than India. In her nightmares, mysterious entities tracked her down and surrounded her like hounds at a feast. Ancient heads without bodies and bodies without heads. Even though they were speaking a language she was not familiar with, she knew what they wanted. They desired to crack open her heart like a pomegranate and scatter her love's crimson seeds across the globe.

She was aware of this, though she was unsure of how.

She wrapped her arms around her slick self and reminded herself, 'They want my affection. She loved him more than the sounds of a lifetime; her husband, Randy, was the object of her devotion. Love was saved for her infant daughter, for whom she felt a greater love than life itself. When she recalled speaking to the horrifying entities, she told them, "Take my love, and you will destroy all things." to chastise them. to drive them out.

She washed away the soap film and turned cautiously, watching not to stumble.

She considered her spouse, Randy. Had two years passed since then? Since their union? Sadly, Randy found himself enmeshed and mistakenly identified as IBM's 007 due to the India project. All that dear Randy wanted to do was use his skills to program computers for IBM's clients; nevertheless, since India and then Peru, IBM has only been asked for Randy's assistance for anything other than his programming knowledge. from those who want him to uncover deception, investigate foul play, or solve a homicide. Was it Fernanda's fault? Maybe.In certain ways.Most likely.Because Fernanda had gained notoriety for all the wrong reasons.

When they got back from Peru, she should never have agreed to do the interview with PEOPLE Magazine. Still, she liked the notion of making her own money from the money they paid. Until she could complete her studies in divination and holistic health, additionally, she obtained the approval of her shaman teacher, Paro, whom she had met in Peru, to do divinations on her own.

Most people would be willing to pay for a divination if it might assist them in making a crucial life decision. Do you think they should marry him or her? Invest in that new home? Put money into the new company? Do they have the proper course? Do they love a faithful person? How are they going to reclaim the priceless love they lost? As a shaman, people would gladly pay for her assistance in making these life-changing decisions. She would be delighted to assist. She wasn't ready yet, though.

Her teacher, Paro, had declined to predict Fernanda's destiny once more. Following the terrible Andean divination. And she got it. It was enough once. Love-filled, devoted to her husband and now a devoted mother, Fernanda was destined to be sacrificed. Whatever the meaning of that was.

She wiped her hands together, squirted Argan shampoo onto her palm, put the bottle back on the shelf, and worked the goo into her thick black hair. She combed her fingers over the lengthy strands and considered it a form of rehabilitation. She looked up at the torrent of water. Suds plumed down her legs, swirled across her front, and rippled over her stretch marks. Her anxieties dissipated as the suds did—a sort of tranquility. The baby's wail followed. Her child. She grinned. Nothing endures indefinitely.

Individuals

Not because her story was the cover story, but rather because of the way her gorgeous face drew attention, Fernanda made the cover of PEOPLE Magazine. Editors were aware that Fernanda's natural Mexican beauty, characterized by her almond eyes, firm red lips, and big cheeks framed by silky black hair, would sell a million copies more than a cover image of a disheveled, disgraced cleric. Thus, they featured a small inset of the priest, whose narrative spanned ten pages, beside Fernanda, whose story spanned only three pages, on the cover.

On page twenty-four, the caption stated, "She was a human sacrifice, by Miam S." The full PEOPLE article may be found here, excluding the photo of an eight-month pregnant Fernanda with her husband Randy, wearing an IBM sweatshirt, peeking out of his study:

Barely six months have passed since twenty-nine-year-old Fernanda Guadelupe de Cortez (her maiden name), a wife and soon-to-be mother from Mexico, fell down a snow-capped mountain in Peru. She narrowly avoided being offered as a sacrifice to the gods by Wari tribe members, who are the ancestors of the Incas and still follow the customs of old to appease the gods. Their shaman told the tribe that she was born to be sacrificed, and they believed him.

She tells PEOPLE, "I never thought I would get off that peak." Since then, I've felt chilly every day. She tightens the handcrafted Peruvian shawl over her as she shivers. A terrible scraping noise that sounds like metal grabbing at rock trembles through the wooden floor and shakes the windows. She looks out their cabin's picture window as it faces the Arkansas woods. "Our business partner Chance is operating the mine," she states. "The crystal mine of quartz. There is a tonne of crystal in the mountains surrounding Hot Springs.

Their journey to Peru many months prior had commenced rather routinely. She accepted her husband Randy's invitation to work with him on an IBM project. But soon after they got there, they learned that the Cuzco bank manager had actually asked Randy to come because his son had been abducted. Randy from IBM had not been employed by him to work on his computer system. Rather, he had employed him in the hopes that Randy would be able to reclaim his little kid.

Randy objected. He was not a very good detective. However, it appeared that news of his accomplishments in India, including stopping a kidnapping, had spread. Reached the bank manager in Cuzco, Peru, who was in need of assistance. Randy was persuaded by Fernanda to look for the man's boy. So they gave it a shot. Before they knew it, they were trekking the rough, rocky Inca Trail accompanied by Wari shamans and porters. Then, high in the Andes, came the fateful divination by the shaman, who said that Fernanda was so full of love that the world could hardly contain her. He said she would be the best human sacrifice in two millennia, the most perfect of all. A little while later, the porters swept Fernanda off her feet. Drugged. Buried in the snow to be claimed by the gods, on the same mountain peak where the Wari sacrificed infants for a millennium. A human offering to Mama Killa, Inti, and all the spirits of the mountains.

Reiterating, "I never thought I would get off that mountain," Fernanda gets to her feet. Her abdomen expands organically, complementing the rest of her voluptuous figure. She gives a fleeting smile. Head shakes her.

QUESTIONS: Has the missing boy ever been located?

She points to the study behind her and says, "Randy, my husband, he asked me not to talk about that." She extends. Her sleek shoulders almost allow the shawl to tumble off. He finds it annoying that I'm conducting this interview. Since our journey to Peru and our honeymoon in India, far too many bizarre things have occurred.

She walks over to the photo window.

Even now, strange things still happen. Mira. Take a look. She gestures towards the two men standing in the underbrush on the nearby hilltop. One is holding binoculars. FBI representatives. The FBI was keeping an eye on me following what occurred in India—murders and disfigurements." Then she hesitated, trying, but failing, to grin. "I was once interviewed by them. They called me the Ripper, Fernanda. I was accused of terrible things.

She is unwilling to discuss what transpired in India any further.

She slides out onto the porch after opening the front door and pushing open the screen. An elderly couple, who each paid ten dollars for the opportunity, excavates newly deposited dirt mounds containing mining tailings. They are looking for crystals that are loose. The sound of the screen door slamming causes them to briefly look up before they go back to their digging, almost as if they are hypnotized.

Bumblebees and honeybees fly around. The scent of turned earth and pine fills the air. The bees' flight is disrupted by the ominous strain of the machine on stone once more.

Fernanda tells about her father, who has always said that she fell from the skies to him when she was a newborn. Her mother was unknown to her. She describes how her father led a mariachi band in her native Mexico. How before she could even walk, Daddy taught her how to play the trumpet. She traveled throughout Mexico on band tours.

When I was seven years old, my father's band took me on a tour of the Chichen Itza ruins. I also got lost. Suddenly, three Mayan men—you know, Indians—showed up, dressed in traditional garb, and offered me gifts prior to my father discovering me.

She examines her hands as though they are those old gifts.

Flowers, she replies. Herbs?With a coin in gold pesos.

She experiences nightmares. Since the time of India.Worse than the Peruvian incident. A spiteful girl tries to persuade her in a recurrent dream that she must die because she is too loving.

She excuses herself and enters at the same moment that Chance, her business partner, emerges in dirty dungarees from the mine. He climbs up the porch stairs. Despite the scar on his face, he has a sunburn, is attractive, and is a strong man.

He touches the scar and explains, "A big cluster I was prying loose one morning released before I was ready."

He claims that Fernanda's pursuit by the FBI is absurd and that she is not guilty. He claims to have known her "since I graduated from high school." "In the trunk of my car, Randy and I smuggled her over the border from Mexico. Did she mention that to you?

He dabs at his forehead. Observe the pair working in the tailings. He spits.

Yes, Randy and I were great friends in Texas during our high school years. To celebrate our graduation, we took my car and traveled to Mexico. He stops to lick his chapped lips. That was the first night that Randy and Fernanda met. He was so infatuated with her that he offered to assist her in crossing the border in exchange for a kiss. Is that really true? Put oneself in jail for a kiss? I also assisted them. But at the time, we were all insane.

Using his sleeve, he knocks out a bee. "We spent some time together. She and I. Years, in fact. She assisted me in opening the mine. After then, Randy got back from Paris. He stops and looks over at the screen door. "They are now married." He glances in the direction of the tailings piles. Tiny sparks occasionally pop out of the ground as sunlight strikes the flawlessly flat faces of crystals that are partially buried. "I also have a husband. Be the father of a son. There is where we reside. Pointing at a barely discernible roof on the opposite side of the mine. He descends the porch stairs first.

He pauses and says, "I used to call her Freddy, though I knew she never liked it."

When people called the FBI to find out why they were pursuing Fernanda, they were told to speak with INTERPOL. When asked if they had any information about a file on Fernanda the Ripper or Fernanda the Innocent, the INTERPOL authorities declined to comment.

Kindly share your thoughts on this topic on the just-launched PEOPLE blog.

The guy and the woman carried on creating a life together as the years went by. They saw that their son developed into a lovely young guy with a lot of talent and promise. Together, they overcame many obstacles, but they always showed each other love and support.

The man and the woman reflected on a lifetime of love and adventure as they marked their 50th wedding anniversary. They were aware that they were fortunate to have had a love that endured and grew more intense with each passing year.

They were appreciative of all the experiences they had had together, as well as all the difficulties and victories they had overcome. They were aware that their love had been the one thing that had supported them through everything and remained a constant in their life.

They knew they were intended to be together forever as soon as they gazed into one other's eyes. Together, they had ridden out life's storms, and each obstacle they overcame strengthened their bond.

The guy and the woman realized they had received a priceless present as they danced and held hands at their anniversary celebration. They had been blessed with a love that would endure forever and support them through all of life's ups and downs.

Thus, with love in their hearts and a resolve to never give up on one other, the man and the lady faced the future with anticipation and optimism, knowing that they would face whatever came their way as a couple.

They were thankful for their love on a daily basis, understanding that it was a rare and valuable thing. They understood that nothing could ever alter their destiny of being together forever.

www.ingramcontent.com/pod-product-compliance
Lightning Source LLC
Chambersburg PA
CBHW052158110526
44591CB00012B/1998